ANUPAMA

First published in 2021 by
BecomeShakespeare.com

One Point Six Technologies Pvt Ltd,
123, Building J2, Shram Seva Premises,
Wadala Truck Terminus,
Wadala (E), Mumbai - 400037
T:+91 8080226699



ISBN: 978-93-90463-97-8

DEDICATED TO

All those who have emerged through darkness

# GRATITUDE

<u>To SAHIB, who was, is and well be present forever</u>

We meet end number of people in life who leave impressions on us. Out of them, few change us and few modify us. The point is that if accepted what happens, everything happens for good. The universe is wise enough to know what we require the most.

In this journey, I cannot forget to thank Osho, who taught me to say YES in every situation and made me believe in a fact that "This too shall pass".

Thank you very much Kahlil Gibran for writing 'The Prophet'. This book gave my thoughts a direction and Mani Bhaumik for writing 'Code Name God' which actually triggered the quest.

I cannot forget to thank Dr. Brian Weiss, who again inherits a belief that we have been together since lives.

Lastly, dear husband, nothing would happen without your support and persuasion.

Anupama, the author of Khoj-The Quintessential Quest is a usual person who believes that whatever happens in life, are not the result of our choices.

In fact the choices are result of our inner and outer circumstances.

As a writer, she says that writing is generally driven by the darker phases, however, if we manage to overcome them, we make a book.

As per her, Khoj is an ordinary compilation of different thoughts and episodes that led her to search herself. The pursuit is still on.

Anupama is a reader, a listener and most importantly, a person stuck in Marshland. She is a Public Relation Professional and has been associated with Mass Media industry before moving to the field of education.

# PROLOGUE

She is always surrounded with disturbing questions. She finds her peace of mind stolen. She in the mirror sees herself broken. She fails to understand why was there so much of darkness? Why was she disordered all the time, even while making smallest choices?

Did not even know what she was looking for.

Will she have her lost horizon back?

Who Am I, why am I and what is the purpose of me being here?

We do not get answers as of course, we are too much engrossed in noise within us? So is she.

The hidden answers remain underneath throughout.

She finds herself amid the marshland, something pulling her deep down but she was determined to fight and overcome. Flourish at the surface, being rooted still in the bog.

The everlasting introspection is what she goes through in this journey, however, finally finds that reverie, to be a total bliss and ecstasy.

# WHO AM I

The prevalent and most disturbing questions that keep on knocking the doors and we keep ignoring are Who Am I? Why am I and what is the purpose of me being here?

We do not get the answers as of course, we are too much engrossed in noise within us? The hidden answers remain underneath throughout.

Whatever our longings are, they are inwardly. Love, devotion, anger, mystery, curiosity, all emerge from within and are supposed to submerge as one 'I'.

This Khoj is not easy, it takes patience, now again it depends on what you search for. All that you are looking for, is technically within you.

Once a Sufi Master was asked 'who guided you in the path?'

Says he, "A dog". He continues, "One day I saw him almost dead with the thirst, standing by the river edge."

'Every time he looked at his reflection in the water, he was frightened, and withdrew the urge to quench thirst because he thought there was another dog'. His own shadow was scaring him to this extent.

'Finally, such was his necessity, that he cast away his fear and leapt one day into the water; at that moment, the other dog vanished'.

The dog found that the obstacle was he himself.

In the same way, we and within us are our own obstacles. We are unaware that within us are our obstacles and possibilities too.

Once a Sufi Mystic Junaid was at the market place and he sees a person holding his cow with the rope. Junaid asks everyone to stop and stay as he wanted to teach people something very important. The crowd gathers. Junaid asks everyone, who was holding the other? The master or the cow, who exactly is the master?

All reply, the master. Yes, visibly they were right as the cow appeared to be under the wishes of its master.

Junaid cuts the rope and the cow runs. Behind the cow does run the master, now again Junaid asks, who was the master?

<u>**What we are holding on is what is holding us.**</u> That is true, but we ignore it. The holdings need to be freed.

It takes time and patience, but we all have the

possibilities.

Early morning, may be at 6:00 AM, she was awake. Just silently looking out of the window. It was still a little peaceful as of now. She knew in an hour's time the whole street, will be crowded. Lots of chitter chatter, vendors, school buses arriving to take the students to school, in a way contributing to brighten their future, at least we think so. Parents dropping the children at respective bus stops, few kiss their children bye and the child smiling climbs the steps, few drag their children and force them to send away.

In both the cases, parents have a kind of satisfaction on their face. They know that it is their responsibility to give their children a better tomorrow. For that they keep on trying their best.

Staring at the road, she was still thinking, does it really decide how it is going to be later.

Does an academic excellence define your future? You may have financial stability, you may have position and maybe some power, however, is that enough for everyone. Does that even matter too for few?

The elders try to still impart what in their understanding is best.

Just like a lizard stuck with the ceiling of a palace feels that she is holding the ceiling, the entire responsibility to keep the ceiling up is her's. If she leaves

**<u>it, the ceiling will fall. She feels the pride of a saviour.</u>**

Poor creature, lives her whole life carrying such a burden on her shoulders.

People already started to gather, it was 7:30 AM now. She also had to get up and get ready to hold her roof on her shoulders.

# THE MARSHLAND

Dense in dawn, the screaming silence...

Scary and scorching heat in the womb of stressed marsh,

The circular motion of spinning world,

All around, there was no way to be out

The bog pulling deep inside,

Beneath the layer of dried leaves was dark stinking substance...

Too sultry to wipe it over,

Realised she later that with what she was wiping was the part of the same bog.

The marsh pulling down to hide her in its depth

Yet she pushing herself out of that dingy waste

It is no more a struggle of superiority or worth,

Still let's see, who wins over as the both have some dearth.

And this Marshland gets you what? Takes you where? What is born of this marsh?

If we have ever visited a Buddha Stupa or Temple, or just that if we remember a painting of

Buddha, we see the flower Lotus around him. Lotus is the only flower that is offered to Buddha.

There is an important message, it is about Buddha's acceptance of all.

A beautiful flower that blooms when stems are in the bog.

Lotus, Buddha's favourite. No it's incorrect. Lotus was not the Gautama Buddha's favourite flower.

Lotus in fact is not just the flower, it is a representation, a symbol of the serenity of that bog pit.

Lotus that flowers in the bog, is a representation of highest form of human consciousness.

A representation of Buddhahood.

Not only in Buddhism is lotus flower regarded, in fact in different cultures it is considered significant in various ways. Particularly in eastern religions, Lotus is considered to be a symbol of purity, enlightenment, self-regeneration and rebirth. Its characteristics are a perfect analogy for the human condition, even when its roots are in the dirtiest waters. Lotus is also a symbol of balance for the same reason, its strong ground in the mud while it blooms on the outer surface of water.

Stalled in suffering of daily life, our spirits start out like a lotus bud, tightly closed and buried deep in the muddy dark-bog. In order to blossom, it make its way through the murky water until it finally breaks the surface and then opens all its petals.

Exactly this is how it happens with human. When you think that you are going through the darkest phase of your life. You are done, you cannot fight any more, you have given up, and you realize that something changes. There is a force that pulls you out of that darkness.

What is that force? -Khoj- The Quintessential Quest.

The possibilities that we see in darkness after giving up is the blooming lotus within us.

Darkness, the dingy substance actually soils the consciousness and strengthens the roots. The warmth of that depressed marsh melts the unconscious fear and insecurities. The silence of that bog pit helps us hear the noise within.

She is just trying to know herself, uncover the real strength and reveal her own identity to herself. There is a sheet of dried leaves, on the upper surface that's thick enough to take quite a long time to be removed.

Yet has to be, once the leaves are removed, then only she will be able to see the light beyond the marshland. This marshland is not the end, rather this is a beginning.

She will make through it, drop the dingy waste, the sticky substance that is soiling her roots, she will come out as a Lotus to embrace the Buddhahood that will help her to accept the dearth of flower and the root both.

When the gloomy phase and brighter days are combined, then they make a journey called life. The lotus is a sign of perseverance and then hope which is a reminder that says to always trust in the uncertainty as that may lead to the light, the right direction.

Journey from a muddy seed to a magnificent blossom offers the hope that something beautiful can grow from the suffering and pain. We too will eventually flower.

She does not have any idea.

The journey she is in seems to be never ending. She sees her darker self in mirror.

Shopping no more gives any pleasure. Feels as if nothing of her holds meaning and there is no substance to life.

Day after the other, in fact moment after moment, she is just breathing. She does not have friends, she does not enjoy going out anywhere. She is equally restless inside and outside is more terrible.

On that day her office mates planned to go out for dinner. It was a celebration of the prestigious award their agency received for their services. This is the time when their firm had reached to the position where the name was enough identified in Advertising and Marketing industry.

The team was supposed to reach in a pub at a particular time.

Despite of being very happy and excited while planning, now suddenly she did not wish to be there. She was happy with the success but did not wish to be a part of noise.

She does not find meaning in any such occasions. She feels lost and empty.

There have been episodes when she wanted to get up from bed, but her body did not move. She found herself freezing and getting numb when she technically was supposed to be active participant. She still remembers that New Year's party. Dressed in beautiful red gown, she was ready to go, rock the floor, groove in joy. She was popular amongst colleagues and friends for her dancing skills. Her colleague arrives to pick her up, as previously planned. However, something happens, she stumbles and sits on the floor. What? She does not know, but she could not take a step forward. This fellow down stairs kept on calling, she did not pick up phone. This person comes up to, keeps on ringing the door bell, she knew it was him, she still does not open the door as she did not have enough strength to walk till the door.

Now this colleague starts banging the door, sounded aggressive. She walks slowly, opens the door tells him that she would not be able to join. He sees that she was all set, ready for the party so asks for a reason and well-being of her. She slams the door. What would she tell him? She just had a bout of panic, and she was feeling endless chaos inside her and at the same time such a dense vacuum. Who will understand these unreasonable causes?

Of course her colleague must have felt disgusted, she could even imagine his expressions. Anyways he leaves. Later on they share the pictures of the rocking night wishing her New Year and with a message that they missed her. For a moment that brought smile on her face, a momentary pleasure and fades. What would be the pleasure that would never casts off? The next question she has.

# EMPTINESS-AN EMPTY ROOM

When you start hearing your own chaos clearly, that is the time, we have knocked on the door of that Empty room that we all have within us. The door opens, however, the void is daunting, petrifying, and we try to find the nearest distraction to avoid the noise that we are suddenly able to hear in that emptiness. It is almost impossible to explain this state, or define it in some set of words as it is different for all.

We are not talking about any spiritual awakening, it is just an opportunity of being one with oneself.

It is a beginning for stronger connection with ourselves, if we are able to live through it. Agreed that it is not at all easy. Unfortunately, no matters how hard we ignore, the door once opened does not close.

We all experience it at some or the other time, however, few name it and few only pass through it.

The divine grace, although scary, it is a state that enthuses the transformation process in a human. It is not an external change, it was always an eternal truth, however, remained unseen unless one day we suddenly found ourselves unacquainted with all the peripheral pleasure. We feel no emotions, neither do we feel creative anymore, we may start disliking ourselves as to find everything we did till date useless. But the point of content is, what did we do? Things just happened, the way the door has opened now, on its own.

Maybe we find ourselves in a state as weak as even to stand for a while becomes difficult. As if all the energy has been squeezed out of us.

You find your gut blank, a widespread darkness to deal with.

We have different experiences while struggling through this phase. When you are in deep sleep, and suddenly wake up to find yourself between nothing, that's emptiness.

When all that you always found interesting, stand useless, that is a signal to tell you that you have proceeded on a journey towards a new discovery.

The one who had excellent sense of humour, suddenly finds bliss in silence, in fact maybe he has lost his humour. The one intelligent brain, finds difficulty in counting digits, an always organized person suddenly does not pick up his wallet while leaving from home.

These can be the result of the transformation process that has silently started within us, without announcement, this sudden change that happens has shaken us a little, however, we are clueless and at the same time helpless.

You feel sick, but there is no returning back, you have potential to move forward, that is why you could reach to that room.

The peace will come through chaos, and accepting what comes is the only way to live through the void.

This Empty room is always there deep inside us, out of sight, often behind numerous doors of materialistic world, ambition, emotion, desires etc.


A commonly heard word, but actually what does it mean? Have you ever felt that whatever  you have in front of you, that lacks meaning in your life? Have you ever experienced, that you wake up in the middle of the night, just to find that you have nothing left.

One fine day, during a regular course of work, you are just blank, as if you do not have a clue of what is to be done the next minute.

If you ever encounter such thoughts, that's a signal

to begin with something not thought of and done ever in your life time.

These feelings bring lots of questions to your mind, however, the point is that no one would be able to answer them. In such situation, what best we can do for ourselves is to let the questions arrive and you accept them in your empty heart.

Emptiness is an opportunity, we need to accept it. Gradually we realize that it was a call for awakening. This is an opportunity to unfold mysteries inside us, believe it or not, it stripes away what we were and introduces us to someone we never knew. It is a seer bliss.

The search, led by your emptiness will work for you as a peeler, you keep on peeling your layers, and you find yourself, and ultimately one day even that self is dissolved in something that is beyond life.

Then your being becomes, Nothing, the ultimate NOTHINGNESS that is to attain.

Hence it is advisable here, do not fear the blank. It is a stimuli.

We fight a lot every time to find some meaning for our existence. Whereas the point is that existence is nothing.

The life being spent in finding your worth, stands unworthy one day when you suddenly feel that one moment of complete void in your gut, just like a dried leaf, you feel floating. Swayed by the wind in its direction, you find yourself aimless and useless.

Useless-ness too is a bliss.  We put too much of efforts to become useful, establish our worth, compare ourselves with our counterparts. Have we ever given a thought to the fact that do we really need to do anything become useless? Nothing.

Being said that, we here are not talking about our karmas. Karmas are pre-decided, we all have our shares, so needless to say, and we cannot avoid it. The real point is, fulfilling your assigned karmas, without any anticipation to prove something and avoidance of self-imposed pressure on ourselves.

When it does not matter, what we achieve then the achievement happens simultaneously. We are not talking about achieving something financial or social. We are talking about the true bliss and peace within us.

Being worthless and useless brings us a pleasure for eternity.  There are numerous beautiful stories and those stories are actually the gist of life.  The experiences of real life that over the period of time worked as path finder and leading light for many.

# USELESSNESS IS BLISS

I have heard a story of uselessness from the Tao.

There was a carpenter in Tibet, a very renowned one, he was traveling across a city. There was a timber tree, a very old, very huge. It was considered as a sacred tree in the temple of the God of Earth. The tree was so large that it could cover a thousands of people in its shade. It was crowded around due to the sacred value that people thought of it. The tree must be hundreds of years old and eighty feet tall. Its branches spread in all directions.

When everyone stood gazing at it, the carpenter, just noticed and walked further. This man had his assistant walking with him, who was completely surprised to see this. He ultimately asked his master that he had not seen such a timber in his entire life. As they were carpenters, the tree was worth their attention, still how come the master did not even stop there? They could have made so many boats, furniture and coffins using the branches of that tree.

On that the master said, forget about it. That tree is not even worth talking, that's how it has attained its age. If you make a boat of it, it would sink, if you make a furniture it would break easily, the doors made of it would sweat. The wood of that tree was of no use and he adds that he had not seen such a useless tree yet.

The carpenter reaches home and when he goes to rest, he has a dream. The dream was about the sacred tree. The tree asks him, why did he compare him saying the most useless one? Did he have any idea how difficult it is to survive if you are useful? Then he tells the carpenter that, if he had been useful, he would been cut and shredded end number of times. To survive with all the original assets it was important for the tree to be useless. This was an eye opener for the carpenter.

**************************************************************************

The trees original virtue is to provide shade to others, to do that, survival was most important. As many times the tree would be cut and trimmed and rugged, it will lose the original virtue. To provide shed to people, is the real karma of a tree. Open branches of a tree invite the clouds to rain and its roots keep the soil together.

Likewise, to prove oneself better than others, we trim and layer ourselves so much that we forget our real self. We have completely forgotten the real purpose.

This feeling of emptiness is an opportunity for awakening. If we start seeing everything useless, we may find our real worth.

We are born with curiosity and question about self. If we can see this whole mystery of life, it will certainly compel us to explore the limits.

To know life, it is important to begin with death.

# GOING BACK TO SELF

What seems to be the end, is just the completion of a cycle. The ultimate destination, the death.

We are aware that once the breathing stops, that is death. But accepting the fact is probably the toughest thing that one could ever think of. The biggest fear of every human.

It is strange that to know the life, it is important to begin with acceptance of death, similarly to understand death, it has to be seen from the heart of life. Life and death are one, they are the two sides of same coin.

We need to understand that the fear of death too has a reason. The most important reason is that we only see others dying. We see the death of our loved ones or the acquaintances. We feel the pain of separation, however, we never still accept that this leaving is for all. We do not see ourselves lifeless, although it is not true if we think in a deeper sense. However, we never are involved in that leaving. We do not see ourselves dead. The outer symptom of death is really scary. The body that we see breathing, celebrating, working suddenly happens to be resting pale lifeless and then converting into ashes or being buried to become the soil. Of course, it is not easy.

We are just the watchers of life till the time we really die.

Acceptance of death happens once you understand that this whole drama of life is temporary and we are simply playing our roles.

Once accepted the death, fear drops. For that to happen, there is a transition required. To accept the self is to be the existence and the existence to be nothing. It is the real phenomena that helps in acceptance of death.

# CHRONICLES OF SHAMSHANA...

Sitting with the burning pyre, I acknowledge the gift

Way it grew and moved towards the end.

The journey was swift

We run innumerable races...wear different faces...

Tarnish each other and create various massacre...

Malign the beautiful present.

Trying to align which is already inherent

Day by day, with passing years...

The greed to "become", shaped itself as fear.

Scared I when reach Shamshana...

I realized this is where lies, Antim Vishram

Today, I am joyous...

I know this last rite is only righteous.

The fearful thought of end, was nothing just a skip of one breathe.

I rest my life which was so futile.

Resting on the pyre. I was just a pile.

Death was the ultimate destination. She had heard it from many. Was it that easy to accept it? If it was so, why does not a man stop struggling to live? The acceptance of end may reduce anxieties and distress of living, however, a man just ignores a pivotal fact and keeps on trying to beautify the futility. Neither the beginning nor end is in man's control; still he tries to control every other incident of his life. Today, she was there to witness a final journey of a body. She was sitting silently as she felt that she was there for a reason. Maybe this was the inclusion of her own life. She was here to have answers of her questions. Her questions about life, about death and about the journey, in her questions itself were the answers.

She agreed that yes, the day we are born, there was no surety about life, however, one thing was sure that the person who is alive in this moment, will be dead in some other time.

She was at the cremation ground. A colleague's father had passed away after a long disease. She knew that the family of deceased was in pain. Her colleague was in tears when she met him at the cremation. Sitting there at the corner she was observing everyone. Yes there were people who were broken due to the loss; however, at the same time they knew that the journey had become so complicated and difficult that everyone wanted an end to it. She heard someone saying, "Good that he is free from the pain." Other person added that "now his family and children would live stress free".

So, that was it. Yes, the end of everything. She was looking at the pyre, as if was able to talk to the body that lay on it. Between the fires was his entire journey and this Mr. Something today was nothing, just a body.

She remembered the initial days, when this body was diagnosed with the disease and how his son, her colleague was sharing his father's struggle with everyone. He looked to be so proud of his father. He just wanted to do whatever possible to prolong his father's life.

But today, things were different and it was genuine because this body had completed its journey, however, others were still in it and finding it difficult to live in that situation.

The person, who spent all his life trying to earn and save for himself and his next generations, did not realize that this all is going to be pointless when it was time for him to leave this world and depart to the other one. She kept on wondering that how we feel that our loved ones would not be able to bare our loss, however, the fact is that it just happens. Everything continues as it was.

It is just a matter of one skip of breath and other side is freedom. Freedom; from the fancies that we were indispensable, independence from all the hustle that we created and traversed through to make things better for us.

How childish is a thought that the bond we share with this world and bodily form is an inseparable tie. It's all so vain, followed by more mysteries about the transition of life after death, known as after life, barely anyone is aware of that.

As an avid reader, she has been reading about astral world, about the conversion of soul from body, about the voyage of life-force. She felt proud of her knowledge, but did it really mean something. What was the purpose of understanding after life, when life itself was unknown? It was the day for more clarity about her persistence.

Death is vital cessation from all the miseries and scuffle. The transformation from a man to body is the final journey. The home, a place for selves that we construct in our entire life, in the end happens to be just a tourist destination. We arrive, play our role, which are pre-decided by the one supreme and then we leave. The final abode is where we reach formless, shapeless and nameless.

Is not this all very simple and clear? We make an appearance, we act, we depart, and then, who is that who is doing all this? Is it us? Who is that we are in control of? Is it us. Who is that who picks up when we fall? Is that some external force or some eternal source, yet to be discovered?

No matters what, death remains <u>The Ultimate destination</u>

# THE FIRST EMERGED FIRE-NACHIKETA-BY PURANAS

Dialogue between Nachiketa and Yama, comes from the later Upanishad.

Nachiketa is known for his rejection of material desires which are short-lived, and for his single-minded pursuit of the path of realizing salvation emancipation of the soul from re-birth.

Nachiketa went to the Death's home, the god of death, Yama. But the god was out, and he waited three days without any food or water. On his return, Yama felt sorry to see that a Brahmin guest had been waiting for really long without food and water at his home. In Indian culture guests are believed to be equal to god and causing trouble to god is a great sin.

In order to recompense or rectify his mistake, to which Yama was not even at fault, Yama told Nachiketa, "As you have waited in my house for three days without hospitality, you can ask for three boons from me". Nachiketa first asked for peace for his father and himself. Yama agreed. Next, Nachiketa wished to learn the sacred fire sacrifice, which also Yama elaborated. For his third boon, Nachiketa wanted to learn the mystery of what comes after death.

Yama was reluctant to answer this question. How could he disclose about something that was a mystery even to the Gods? He asked Nachiketa to ask for some other blessing, and offered many materialistic benefits.

But Nachiketa replied that material things will last only till tomorrow- What an eye-opener. Nachiketa who knew the futility of materialistic world.

He who has encountered Death personally, how can he desire wealth? No other boon would do. Yama was secretly pleased with this disciple. He hence, elaborated on the nature of the true Self, which persists beyond death. The key of the realization is that this Self is inseparable, the supreme spirit, and the vital force in the universe. Yama's explanation is a succinct explication of Hindu metaphysics.

Yama emphasizes that goal of self is to realize Aatma, which is real self. Aatma that is omnipresent, formless, smaller than the smallest and larger than the largest.

After death, it is the Atma that remains; the Atman is immortal. The reality is discriminating soul from body,

body is mortal.

Thus having learned the wisdom of the Aatma from Yama, Nachiketa was freed from the cycle of births.

According to Hinduism, since fire is considered to be one of the holy & pure elements, Puranas name the first emerged fire as Nachiket

Knowing the death is not about freeing oneself from the end of life, but attaining to something which is purer than life. The eternal, once realized, it leads to acceptance of the end and the new beginning starts. That's what is the crux of this communication between Yama and Nachiket. Nachiketa knew that all the things in this world are temporary and he was not afraid of death. He understood that following the path of truth is the gateway to heaven.

# AMBITION-STRUGGLE BETWEEN SUCCESS AND FAILURE

As the perfect arguments cannot be given name, so cannot be perfect success or failure. It is mainly the prospect and opinion.

If we think of success, we are continuously thinking of failure too as the thought of success itself is not a fact.

We alone are not the ones chasing success, there are millions and we are just one of the crowd.

The hunger to succeed is bringing us more misery and discontent. Huge ambition is taking away the peace of mind, and we are in a continuous race.

One fine day, suddenly to realise that what we considered to be the success, was not really the one. Standing on the top most ladder, we find the ladder being re constructed. While we were standing on the step, trying to look downwards with pride, someone from the crowd already succeeds in climbing few more steps to reach the higher position.

So there is no limit of success, hence the expectation to succeed is false, right from the emancipation of thought.

Similarly if you fail, then too you are unaware that the failure was just an opportunity for you. You just could not grasp it correctly. Decoding failures too is a skill. Every failure has a mantra of success hidden at the core. However, as it is so difficult for humans to accept the failure that we seldom invest time in analysing it. Although, there are case studies that state that in case failures are evaluated, they certainly bring a plan for success.

The failures are charge free tuition of success. If we learn from them the chances of repeating mistakes reduce and one blunder is still ok, however, the repetition of same ones are no more mistakes. Past failures teaches us about adversities and our responses to them in clearer manner.

True leaders understand that no matter how accomplished they may be, failures can still teach them something. Not everyone can be as modest to go through self-analysis, after a failure. We need to learn to take failures positively, the key to success is also in failure.

Having spoken about key to success, very important

point is that key to living is accepting success and failure both as part of life. A process.

It is just like, nothing fails as fast as success, the desire of success that did not let you sleep peacefully, after achieving it, you are still struggling to have more of it. To maintain it.

This greed, actually converts us into someone else, we fight, we struggle, and we fake, just for one misconception of success.

The point of thought is that neither the success nor is failure. Success comes and goes and so does failure.

The difficulty is that we do not understand what ultimately success is. Success should be something that helps us evolve as a human, it has no strings to any position or materialistic benefits. Success is when us can feel compassion towards the creation and when us have gratitude towards the creator.

In the race of success, we dropped the soul, and it is the body that's one day going to be tired. Let's now halt and find our lost soul.

It is a truth that no matters what you achieve you will be miserable in any case, if you do not find yourself.

She reaches her office, on the way listening to music, she was trying to keep her focus on planning the agenda for meeting she was to head today.

Her team was working for quite long on preparing the presentation, assembling the data to prove how the agency could have been helpful for the brand building of the client.

Yes the brand, the client that the agency wanted on board and the expectation of this brand was such that brought lots of pressure to the whole team.

She too was feeling quite stressed and anxious.

The main reason for this anxiety was her record. The performance record for her said that she had never lost a client in any of her pitches.

She was dynamic and understood the psychology of business fraternity. She understood the market trend and worked accordingly to pitch the clients during business meetings and not only bringing in, she also sustained on their expectations with her strategic planning and marketing skills.

The branding agency she worked for had the reputation of establishing brands in their respective industries and she was their one of the most efficient Client Servicing Manager.

Till date, since last three years, whosoever joined in, she was a role model for all.

This time she was a little scared, since this client had called in all top notch branding agencies to bid and they were to make selection depending upon the offerings by each agency.

Since this project was assigned to her, she along with her team worked day and night to get in all appropriate and exciting data together. Many a times she lost patience and calm, yelled at her subordinates.

She had a gut feeling that her team was going to be defeated in this bidding and she worked more anxiously and furiously in order to eliminate the chances of defeat.

With an assumption of this failure, the fear was something else. She used to see herself walking through the workstation and all her colleagues and subordinates talking behind her back.

She probably at times heard such gossips in her imaginations.

So this was the real reason of fear.

More than defeat, she was scared of facing people. In her imaginations, she had seen her tarnished image into their eyes, she even saw herself being thrown out of her strong position and someone else replacing her.

Now this someone was already her enemy in her imagination, whereas, this character was just imaginary till now.

Ultimately it was the day. She reached for meeting along with the team of her two associates.

While entering, ten minutes prior to the time allotted to them, she saw another team exit. She felt goose bumps in her gut.

She was about to flip on staircase while climbing up, her subordinate helped her to stand strong.

Now it was their turn to present what they had to. They entered and took their seats. It was a time for deal, the client looked satisfied, and they shook hands and left leaving the proposal on conference table.

On the way back her subordinate asked her, was she alright? This question took her to an hour back, to the conference room.

While presenting her slide, she had gone numb. She fumbled and started sweating badly. There was a pin-drop silence at both the sides, however, suddenly her subordinate took it over, presented the rest of the slides, confidently like a pro. In an organized manner, he started by explaining that probably she was little unwell and asking for permission to take the meeting further. To which, he was granted the authorization.

He closed the meeting. Meanwhile she kept on observing him, how well he had taken up all the required skills.

Sitting in the cab, on his question, first thing was

she appreciated him for his efficiency and confidence. On which, he says, whatever he has learnt was all from her. The other colleague added that she has always been a trainer and a leader in true sense.

She closed her eyes and tried to relax. For a moment now it was not that important for her to get the deal.

I-Pad beeps, she checks her E-mail and there was a confirmation mail from the client side congratulating them to making the deal.

They reached office, her supervisor was waiting for her to pat on her back, but this time she puts her subordinates forward because on the way back she had learnt to **share success and making space for others to walk-in.**

In fact, now this lesson she felt was a true success as this pressure of winning all the time had made her almost crazy and insane and ultimately she ends up doubting her own calibre in process of proving her potential all the time.

Today she knew that there was no limit to it and suddenly how this deal stood so futile to her. Although it was her work, she would continue to do that in all her capacities but may be now  onwards, she will work for herself, not for anyone else to approve her. Not at all with a pressure to win.

She smiled with pride, patted her subordinates and acknowledged them in front of all saying that it is the team that makes a leader, as strong as the leader makes the team.

Today she understood, she had potential to guide and groom, be a light.

Till now whatever she did, was pulling her into her own darkness.

What exactly she missed in her life was a bigger question.

But this was not over yet. Nothing finishes, incidents happen, we feel liberated, we feel burdened, then we again forget as the life continues, the struggle continues and the yearning continues till the time we do not reach to the ultimate realization.

Again the question is, what is that realization?

# THIEF, THE MASTER

Lost his way in a forest, Junaid once reached the nearest village that he could find, it was midnight. Everybody was fast asleep. He tried to find shelter for the night, until finally he found one man. He asked him, 'It seems only two persons are awake in the town, you and I. Can you give me shelter for the night?'

The man said, I can see from your gown that you are a Sufi monk and I feel a little embarrassed to take you to my home. I am perfectly willing, but I must tell you who I am. I am a thief. Would you like to be a guest of a thief?

For a moment, Junnaid hesitated. Seeing that, the thief says 'Inviting you means danger, but I am not afraid. You are welcome. Come to my home. Eat, drink, go to sleep, and stay as long as you want, because I live alone and my earning is enough. I can manage for two persons. And it will be really beautiful to chit-chat with you of great things. But you seem to be hesitant?'

On hearing this, Junaid seemed to be humbled. The thief said, Come on! He fed the Sufi, gave him something to drink, helped him to prepare for sleep and he said, now I will go. I have to do my own thing. I will come back early in the morning.

Early in the morning the thief came back. Junaid asked, Have you been successful?

Now the reply of this thief was a lesson. He says, "Not today, may be tomorrow."

And this happened continuously, for thirty days, every night the thief went out, and every morning he came back empty-handed. But he was never sad, never frustrated—no sign of failure on his face, he always looked happy and said, it doesn't matter. I tried my best. It can happen tomorrow if it has not happened today.

Junaid remembered the thief as one of his greatest Masters. Without him he would not be what he happened to become. As in the journey of realization there were times when he wanted to give up, those times he remembered the thief.

This was amongst the very important stories that Junaid left for his followers and disciples.

Failure happens only when we stop trying.

She is very excited today. Just checking time again and again.  All packing done, she has packed her comfortable pairs of clothes in a bag pack. She has rented a car for two days. It is Friday, she is leaving for a short solo trip. This was a time to treat herself with a brief vacation.

She has been working continuously day and night, maybe twenty hours a day.

She deserved this break. All the plans were set, stay booked. She just waited for the day to end so that she could start on. It was her solo trip after long time, of course she deserved this happiness.

That day, she knew that she did not work at all, even that was fine. One should allow oneself little bit of cheating. One thing that was bothering her again and again was that if last minute meeting comes up for the day, that too unavoidable, she would get late to start. She was to drive self, she did not wish to be late. Although, her destination was just 4 hours away, still she wanted to start sooner.

Now she was so much engrossed in this thought that probably she invited such situation unknowingly.

She, at 4:00 PM receives an E-mail for an urgent meeting with the board members which was unavoidable. It was regarding the budget and appraisals of staff members.

She had to be a part of this meeting. However, during this entire meeting, she was lost in thoughts of her trip. Anxious of driving off roads in dark, crossing unknown roads alone scared her to the extent of panic.

She neither could focus, nor could contribute anything much in this discussion.

The car arrives sharp at 5:00 PM as per her plan.

The meeting closed at 7:00 PM, she was already late. She starts finally on her trip, by now feeling tired, yet plays her favourite song and starts driving, feels better.

She reaches her destination and checks in to the resort, was literally tired so fast asleep.

Next day morning when she wakes up, removes curtains and was awestruck. The view from her room was so serene and beautiful and at the same time, thrilling as the resort was on the top corner of a hill.

She was very happy. Prepares tea for herself interestingly she enjoys the sound of boiling water in the electric kettle of that hotel room. She relishes the aroma of tea and goes out for stroll.

The small hill station, very less popular seemed to be heaven on earth for her. She realized how much she needed this.

While on walk, she happens to re-collect the highlights of yesterday's meeting, and ridiculous that she was now even thinking of that such a futile thing. She was already in between something she was craving for since long. She negates the thought by serving herself with another. She plans for paragliding seeing the advertisement. Her heart fills with another thrill. She spoke to the concerned person and goes to the place. She reaches the hill top, being helped by the instructor to reach the at location. Fastening the guards, tying the parachute etc. when the instructor was sharing tips, she suddenly felt her heart sinking as she had numerous thoughts like what if something goes wrong, the parachute does not rise or inflate. Many such weird thoughts. And then there was a push, just like a machinery, she did that all was required and then, she was now supposed to take the leap of blind faith, she could not. What next? She was pushed, her heart pounded, for once though and after that, it was such a beautiful feeling of liberation, freedom, flying in sky amazing. That's how probably a bird pushes her babies from the nest. Similar feeling she had now.

After some time of that freedom, what next, again back to office. In the sky, her thoughts were so strong that they took her to a day prior, to the conference room, budgeting starts in mind now.

# ARE YOU READY? - ZEN WAY OF CELEBRATION

A popular Zen saint was breathing his last, In Zen tradition, death is considered as a biggest celebration of life. As he was a popular master, he had huge number of followers and disciples. There were a lot of estimations and speculations about his successor. The most worthy, the one who is eldest one, likewise, many guesses.

Crowd was waiting for his last message, the last teaching, and announcement of his successor.

Suddenly the master asks 'Who is ready to come along with me?'

There was a pin drop silence amongst his disciples.

Of course no one would be ready to accept death and even if it comes from the master.

Suddenly a little child gets up and says "I am ready master. I will come with you."

The master says, he is my successor. He is ready. The

one who is ready to die is ready to live.

It was surprising for all as he was the youngest disciple of all. However, master's last words are like sermon.

Talking about sermons, there is another beautiful story about a Zen master who was on his death bed. Again all his disciples were around him waiting for his last words.

There was a complete silence outside, however, the master knew that this silence was only at the surface. Inside, every one present over there had some chaos, lots of thoughts, and eagerness. They just wanted to hear those last words before master left his body.

And the master raises his right hand, point finger towards roof, yet again stays for a moment silent and then says, 'Stop' listen to the sound of squirrels. Then everyone present there realized that there were two squirrels playing on the roof. Making some eccentric noise. Although soothing, yet as they all had so much of chaos inside that they could not realize the beauty of that moment.

-

As per Zen, Last words of master are the direction, a representation of master's journey.

Here the sermon was, 'Be present in the moment'.

Most pious feelings like love, devotion or affection

happens only in present. Anger also happens in present however, is driven by the past memories or experiences and in the same manner anxieties are result of bothersome for future.

Live in present

# WHEN I MET MY OTHER MINE

With my closed eyes, I saw my other mine peeping...

I thought it was hallucination, or maybe I was sleeping...

Gazed, I when at it...She did at me too

..The two mine of my smiled, I realized they were glued...

The thought that emerged said this is the reality. Unless they are together, there is no sanity.

I sat while my eyes were closed...

Truly I Was amazed and dozed...

I saw an adorable moment where..., the allurement and strength walk together...

Kindness and bravery were dancing hand in hand. Realized I this was a lovely bond

Thoughts galloping from happiness to divine... I know, I am incomplete without my other mine.

She once again looked at the mirror.  She was convinced and confident about herself. She had always proved herself to be an asset to the organisation. Her team mates believed in her potentials and they enjoyed working with her. The seniors acknowledge her creative abilities and dedication towards her work. She knows one thing that works for her is the determination to excel in all the projects that she takes up. Out of all, she is the one who has the elite business clients alloted to her. She is the first choice of business associates. For last three conjecutive years she has been winning the recognition as a best performer. The trophies placed nicely aesthetically  on a elevated shelf in her cubicle gave her a feeling of immense content. She planned to work even harder to stay on the top of the list of top performers.  Forgetting herself was one prime thing she did after reaching her workplace.

But after reaching home, she always felt an emptiness. She failed to understand what was the reason behind this. After an accomplished day, why she had restless nights? Every morning, waking up with passion to excel however every evening sleeping with the feeling of emptiness. All her achievements stood void in those hours. In the silence of night, she always heard her heart saying that she was not doing enough for herself. But what was insufficient? She had no clue about it. She at times felt herself laughing at her workoholic approach. Her skills that were praised in those hours of her excellent performance, her lonely hours  proved them to be of no use. At work, she could manage a large group of people, control them and get what was expected from them. However, At  home she did not recognize herself. She was not able to understand her own turmoil, how did she manage to lead her team for projects. These questions had started irritating her to the madness.

Gradually, this hollowness kept aggravating. She started loosing interest in going for work. Her trophies did not motivate her anymore.

Where was it going to end? She had every thing one could think for, but suddenly she did not want them anymore.

This morning she woke up with a shooting pain. She tried to get up and reach to the washroom as she felt as if she will puke. She almost dragged herself in. When she stood infront of the washbasin, which was near the window she saw a shadow of herself. The shadow looked so tiny and lean. She couldnot even relate it to her. Quickly she came out and tried to reach her bed. Laying on the bed, she was still engaged into the thoughts of her shadow that she had seen in the washroom. The series of thoughts start again. She realized that no matters, what she did. No, matters how successful she had become at her workplace, all her achievements kept aside, she was still the same.  No one knew her inside her own house. "Did she herself?" was the another question she had in mind. She tried to pull the thought out, however she could not. She once again tried to get up and get ready for work. The "to do list", actually swayed in front of her eyes. She remembered how much she had to finish. She swallowed the tablets to help her headache and left for work finally.

Moving towards her workstation, with heavy head, walking slowly, she was feeling as if she did not wish to go there that day. She still pushed herself, checked her appointments and started completing the presentation. Like every other day, she started making it better, trying to put things in a perfect manner. Making it very impressive to ensure  a successful business dealing. In all this, she forgot about her headache and the morning hustle.  She started enjoying the day. Met all her day's deadlines and pursued the handy projects further. Had lunch with her colleagues and sat for a small session of chit chat over the cup of coffee in the later evening.  Discussed another day's plan with her team mates and updated about all the developments to her superior. She booked a cab and started for home. She felt happier today as she was glad of ending the day well, which had not started very good. She reached her destination, her  home.

She was hungry, and for a change, wanted to cook for herself. She entered her kitchen to check for grocery and started cooking dal rice for herself.

She played a soft music on her phone and started enjoying the peace she felt inside her after a long time. Engrossed in the music she started recollecting various incidents of the whole day. Traveling through the memories, she again reached to the morning. She felt as if her shadow was standing near her once again, smiling at her.

She heard the whistles of pressure cooker and realized that the dal would have been cooked and overcooking will spoil the taste. What a moment of realization it was! She could connect how over thinking was spoiling her days and nights. She had lost her peace of mind. She was always occupied cooking and boiling her own thought. She was a witness to the reality that how her own contemplations got her so much of suffering as she was paying too much of attention to them.

After eating few spoons, she kept away the plate into the sink and went on to her bed. She knew it was again going to be a sleepless night struggling with herself.

Morning, she informed in the office that she was going to take a day off.  For an employee, who had worked almost every day with equal enthusiasm ,everyone at work was surprised.

All this emotional fight, sleepless nights and gone down appetite had made her really weak.  She could not find any one with whom she could have shared her concern. Her disoriented thoughts were making her wrathful.

She had heard it somewhere that if you have vague thoughts that are difficult to decode, write them and you will find the source.  She started doing so, trying to encounter herself. Whatever came to mind, she started making note of it. Going back again and reading them again and again helped her to connect with herself. She stayed at home for another four days. In this she realized that her work and her achievements had become so important to her that she had left everything behind. Not a moment of fun, not a minute of peace with self, no friends and even distant ties with family, she couldnot realise how badly she needed these all. She was deriving pleasure from her success, but that was not enough for the peace with self. She had stopped spending time on self. On the sixth day of her being on leave, she received a call from work. She was by now supposed to join back as there were lots of backlog accumulated to be cleared.

For once, she thought that she would stay home for few more days. She called her boss to discuss but then she thought she should meet and have a conversation. It was after almost a week that she went out of her home. The morning  breeze, she found to be really soothing. She was casually walking towards her floor, and she realized that the corridor was  well kept and tidy. It always was, the watcher had changed. She had always been so much in hurry to meet her targets and deadlines that she couldnot acknowledge. Today she was at peace, despite of the pressure of backlogs, challenge to ask for more leaves, she still was feeling happier.  She entered her office, the place she had spent years working day and night, today seemed so different, fresh. She went on to her workstation, checked E-mails, a huge pile of them she had waiting. She responded in the required ways. Planned agenda for further actions.

However, there was a slight difference today. She was not in hurry, she did not try to push herself against time. She was not commanding or dominating. She was now performing, her duties. Guiding her team to develop further agenda. The day ended and she was packing up for home thinking she would now go and talk for some more time. She went to the restroom and saw herself, she looked happy and blissful. She realized that basically she was lacking balance in her life. She did not anymore wanted leaves, she was not anymore worried of her thoughts. She had found the source and knew the reason. She had now acknowledged that all the ambition cannot be pursuaded if we lack peace. Success doesnot have any worth, if it doesnot bring happiness and bliss to oneself. Both the aspects went hand in hand and together.

# THE TOO TIGHTENED STRINGS

Once Buddha was meditating under the tree, on the bank of river. Those were the days when Buddha was living in complete hermitage. Abandoned all basic necessities that were required for survival, even food. He ate just one grain of rice in 24 hours, drank only rainwater. Abandoned sleep completely and even it is said that he used to hold breath as much as possible. This whole thing was an attempt to overcome the mind's state of pain and overcome the bodily desires of comfort. He had stopped talking and only meditated.

That day there was a musician, a sitarist who was sailing on a boat with his pupils in the same river where Buddha was meditating. He was explaining an important lesson related to Sitar to his people which Buddha overheard.

His lesson caught Buddha's attention. The lesson was, if you tie the strings of sitar too tight, they will snap. If you tie too loose, they will not produce music.

Hence, an example was music, however, this master was teaching his disciples about the balance in life, this lesson was as important that it even benefitted Siddhartha on the way to become Gautama Buddha.

His six years of abandonment and wandering did not give him much result unless one day, living by the hermitage, he was about to lose his life. Abandoning food made him so weak that in attempt to cross the river, he was about to be drowned and suddenly this lesson by the sitarist arrived as a way ahead. Siddhartha realized that he required balance in his life. He then discovered Middle Way, which later he preached.

Later, when Buddha started to sit for discourses and established Sangha, one day Sona, a son of a rich businessman arrived to listen to Buddha's discourse at the vulture peak. After the discourse, he asked for ordinance as a monk, and he was accepted by the Buddha.

The journey to monkhood started for Sona, who was until now unaware of the sufferings and pain. He was unaware of the scarcities as well, he had what he wanted and desired. Now it was the desire of attainment, realization.

He started the journey and went on it very hard on

himself for the desire of mindfulness.

However, he realized later that his practices were not giving him the desired results, he was disheartened.

Hearing about his sufferings, Buddha spoke to him and gave him the same lesson of mid-way, with an example of Veena that Sona used to play. The too tightened or too loosened strings do not produce music. Sona understood as he too was a musician.

In this journey, today she has also discovered the same lesson. As she was too much engrossed in fulfilling her ambitions for victory and retaining the position, she had lost herself. She fought very hard to retain on top, which she successfully could also to some extent, however, in the process, she lost her connection with herself. She had trouble listening to her own voice. May be she has today found herself once again.

This incident from the life of Gautama Buddha, is an eye opener to all of us.

Buddha was not a Buddha unless he found ease in his lifetime with all the feelings and emotions. He also went through all that is said to be the negative traits.

We all are aware of the day when Buddha was enlightened, however, the attainment of Buddhahood cannot be a day or one incident. It was a journey that we all go through.

Surely in every manner it is a truth that we have seven prime emotions. This seven is coincidentally a very important number.

Seven rishis, Saptrishi Mandal, part of the constellation, seven emotions make human, seven colors are primary that make rainbow, and seven prime notes make sargam, ultimate music. No one remains untouched with the seven bhav. These are universal. Anger, fear, disgust, surprise, happiness, sadness and contempt, all these are there within every human. We may accept or deny, however, the truth is that neither suppressing works nor does hiding. Important is to understand and acknowledge them as your own part.

Again, there is one more angle to it. All the emotions merge in one, it is just that at one moment we are compassionate, other we are cruel. One moment we feel waves of love and another we are dry and barren land. That's a transition that keeps on going, influenced by external sources, however, the fact is all this is internal. Nothing comes from outside.

We all are gifted by the sense of curiosity and questions, however, few of us live ignorant and few realize that quest and try to unfold the mysteries.

<u>For her, she is able to hear the questions, but unable to settle with them.</u>

At times, she feels that the ignorance is a bliss, the quest is not something easy. The one who starts on the journey of unfolding, undergoes lots of confusions and chaos.

Real challenge happens when we try harder to reject the chaos and find peace. While the key is in accepting the chaos, eventually that transcends into the bliss.

As the Buddha talks of Middle way, the balance, that's the key. Although now finding that balance becomes a target and then we find another imbalance. Basically finding is the concern. Finding something which probably does not exist.

Instead, can we look at the situation where we stop finding and start accepting ourselves.

The art or skill of doing something in accord with the essential nature of the thing, simply to sip water when you feel thirsty, dance when you wish to and when you feel like. You can drink your glass of wine and also the green juice when your body needs it. Be brave to accept if sadness endears and laugh even if it's silly, still if you wish to.

She tells herself, let's move and standstill, embrace all our sides.

# WHIRLPOOL

Lost in the whirlpool of stormy desert,

Whirling in your remembrance,

Life left the body...

On trying to hold it tight, says it

The soul that's missing, Is the only origin,

Until you find it keep, breathing...

Will I be back, when the storm calms,

The sand is moist and

Cactus is fragrant

# SKY NEVER FALLS

She was lying on the floor, not unconscious. Just lifeless.

Yes at least she felt so. She was on call with her mother. She had an argument with her. The topic has been same for quite some time now. Her mother wanted her to get married. Not that she was against getting the concept of marriage, she was just not prepared for the complete surrender. She did not know how to convince herself to share her life with anyone else while she had always kept herself too much private.

She had very less friends, out of which, most of them were just to share occasional greetings.

She had her share of mood swings, confusions and curiosity that made her crazy.

She knew that by now, taking the control of entire life on her own shoulders, it was almost impossible to make any adjustment with herself. Moreover to take a second citizenship in life.

These were bigger problems, to her, even sharing her home with someone was a challenge, and she felt she would not be able to. In fact not only felt, she knew it was not possible.

She remembers, once, she had planned a get together with her colleagues at her home.

In her own comfort zone. Still, after a time she started feeling suffocated.

Inner noise in solitude was still bearable.

Her inner self always knew she was holding much of negativity, non-acceptable emotions, for she herself could not accept her misery.

# BLACKOUT-A RENDEZVOUS WITH SELF.

It is scary, darkness is frightening. To conquer it, again the way is through acceptance. Acceptance of the infinite darkness, accepting the recurring blackouts. Most importantly, recognizing our stoppages.

Well, of course, invention of electricity is an example that had not happened if darkness was not scary, we might not have tried to illuminate our lives. However, did that actually irradiate us? It did, outwardly. For inwards it is still our own struggle.

On closing our eyes, at times it happens that we hurriedly try to distract ourselves, the closed eyes puts us face on face with the darkness inside us.

It so happens for few of us that with open eyes also we start seeing those pestering blackouts.

Pouring tea for yourself, you find your hands shaking. While on walk in the breezy beautiful morning, you forget the way back to home, trust me it is not Alzheimer always.

Sometimes, it is awakening to your darkness, when engrossed in your thoughts, we get stuck at a corner, completely confused of what next.

That's surely is a terrible moment. You are clueless of the reason, pathless and fearful.

It is an alarm, let's try to take it positively, every moment of that infinite darkness, we overcome is a step ahead towards an encounter. A rendezvous with self.

Since the time unknown, darkness is considered as an evil, whereas to some, it is an opportunity. Darkness is integrally our inseparable part.

Both darkness and illumination, being the cycle of day and night were created by the creator with a purpose. Similarly our inwardly light and dark, both have their purpose and role in our personal growth.

Here again, we are not talking about spiritual growth. It has already been said that we are born with chances to attain Buddhahood, and as per Gautama-The Buddha, it is all dependent upon being the light unto ourselves. Hence, let's discover that hidden self, first. For that, we need to acknowledge that voltage fluctuation is a part of journey.

Gradually these fluctuations and blackouts will precede to the stillness, when you start finding yourself, amid the dark night always, even at the 12 noon, and then the same blankness, the infinite gloom within you and you become witness to it. This is an opportunity for acquaintance with the ultimate, in depth being of self. The roots.

Finding yourself, is an ecstasy and darkness is your best friend in this discovery. May the blackout leads us to that eureka moment of- A rendezvous with self.

Accept your vulnerability, for your vulnerability is an ultimate strength.

# LIFE LEAVES THE BODY OR WE STOP LIVING FOR THE FUTILE REASONS

She was searching for an important document. Her matriculation certificate. She always had a habit of keeping things organized and well placed in folders. All her documents and files were nicely tagged which made it easy for her to find the stuff when required.

All the containers in her kitchen were tagged and she ensured that everything goes in to the particular container it belonged to.

No one at her workplace ever saw her workstation unorganized, no matters how occupied she be.

One of her subordinate, once placing a pen stand, did not place it in a manner she used to do always, she really yelled at him.

She had all the important dates, targets and deadlines, projection and placements on her tips.

But what was wrong today? Why was not she able

to find that document? It was her home, she only had placed things in her organized manner, and there were no chances of struggle finding it. She tried to remember when was it last when she saw that piece of paper, however, she could not recollect which irritated her. She was fuming on herself, at this time she knew, she had no one else to put the blame on.

For a moment she wanted to kill herself or punish ruthlessly, thankfully she did not.

She was worried also as finding it was very important for her as she was planning to apply for something where she had to attach a copy of all her certificates.

Now her mind starts working very fast. She sees herself failing to join the course that she deadly wanted to pursue to sharpen her skills and to upgrade herself. To add on that anxiety, she sees herself being replaced by someone more competent than her at her workplace. Till date she was bossing around, now she had those colleagues making fun of her.

Another pressure was of getting the certificate re-issued, placing an FIR against it, and going to police station for it. Visiting her home town, her school to get a provisional one for reference and then CBSE headquarters to have the certificate.

She could imagine herself running from one place to another.

She was more anxious thinking all this. To her already disturbed state of mind, this was very difficult to hold her breath and calm down. She finds her nerves collapsing with anxiety and anger. She tries to drink some water. While filling the glass, her hand shook and she dropped the glass breaking it. Tiny pieces of glass, looked like herself to her, she was clueless about why she felt this hopeless. It was ultimately just a paper. The smashed pieces probably helped her to gather herself and diversion of thought from certificate to pieces relaxes the anxiety for document and brings a thought that she has to be careful else she may get hurt.

She collects the pieces of glass, puts them in the trash bag. For all that's shattered, trash bag was the home, she felt.

She then leaves everything and lays on her bed. Struggling with the jumbled thoughts and memories of incidents of her anger bouts which occurred with or without significant reason.

She again has lots of questions like does everyone go through such incidences of anger? Does anger make them lose their calm.

She was now thinking, why does she forget that anger is temporary, the way is compassion for her as of now. Why does she reacts in such a severe manner. Why she ends up humiliating others in that temporary situation and now she was doing the same with herself.

With all her qualities, this emotion of anger was her weakness that pulled her down many times. Her own team, that loved and respected her as a guide and supervisor, they actually were fearful of her anger.

Today's incident was something that ridiculed her A piece of paper made her mad. Or maybe it was not because of the paper, it was that she was angry with herself as she thought that she would never make such silly mistakes. She owned pride in her for her organizational and managerial skills.

The anger is the one that feeds on our own ego. Anger alone can never survive nor can ego, these are complimentary emotions associated with the self and on top of all we are always either ignorant or on denial of it.

Anger is an outcome of exaggeration of incidences which we do in our mind. Ego is an exaggeration of self, a state were see ourselves as little extraordinary.

If a mistake happens, why struggle with self. It is fine to make a mistake, if it happens by others, we again struggle with self in process of punishing or humiliating the other.

Instead if we just accept the fact that, whatever happens, happens for a reason. The anger will vanish and so will ego.

If we are capable enough to spend some time just to look at the moment when we see the rush of anger is us, we may overcome the emotion, though temporarily. After that moment, it often happens that what made us so angry, was not even that relevant to waste energy upon.

Having said that it is not about suppressing the anger, if we do so, it is still going to remain inside us, harming us. Like a fungi to the plant.

Realizing and observing the source is important and then accepting one instead of struggling to suppress or eliminate.

Acceptance is like confession, once made you are

free. You feel lighter.

It is not important to lead a life as perfectionist, rather living is important. It is in fact good to have non-sequential life instead of a set pattern. It is fine to place a mug on the corner of the table instead of center, even if it breaks by falling. If that falling still makes you angry on yourself, only one to suffer is you.

Let's not struggle, accept our anger also completely, it will stop feeding itself on its own.


*There was a samurai warrior in Japan. A very brave and popular, however, he had a weakness, everyone has. He got angry very easily. His opponents knew that and they played this as a technique to defeat him. It worked, as an angry man fails to see the other side of story unless the moment does not pass.*

*Gradually, the samurai started realizing it and might have discussed with someone close. Right from here, the journey had started for him because acknowledging your weakness is not at all easy.*

*So this friend of his suggests that he should learn Zen techniques to overcome his anger. He finds a master and reaches to him.*

*On meeting him first he asks one question to the master, the question was, Master what is difference between heaven and hell?*

*The master fumes and he humiliates the samurai by saying that how dare he even get there, how dare he ask that question and could not he see that master was busy in something very important? He was in the middle of work.*

*And that triggers the samurai. He starts yelling back saying how dare master talk to him like that? Did he even know who he was? He takes out his sword and says that he will cut the master's head right away.*

*And the master says, look son, this is hell, astonished by the statement, the sword drops, and the master says. Welcome to the heaven.*

*Journey started, but was not easy. It was to take time. Whether heaven or hell, both are part of us, we make them, ultimately it's us.*

She was still in bed laying and staring at the ceiling. She thinks, if for a moment she fails to find the certificate, was that a big deal? Yes it might have taken some time, some follow ups, some rounds of visit, but is not she capable of making them?  Of course she was.

About the course she wanted to apply for, she could do it later as well. The moment this thought arrives, something clicks and puts smile on her face, she feels silly of herself. To apply for it she just needed a scan copy and to arrange for it, she only needed to speak to the HR or organization as she already had it in her office records. As it is to pursue anything additional during work, she required an NOC, she anyways had to talk.

So the moment panic and anger subsides, there is an option, a way out. It was always there, earlier she was blinded by her anger and self judgement.

Now she could see the other side.

This mind truly was a dangerous master, and it is worth giving a thought to the fact that how we become slaves to it. Just a moment back, for her it seemed as if the world ended. Now suddenly she had hope, she found a way to resolve the issue from where the anger for self was rising which could have made adverse effect on others too, people, surroundings etc.

But now with the awareness of solution, the anger starts subsiding, and peace replaces the anxiousness. <u>The moment of harmony within self.</u>

# PROFUSELY BEARDED, WIDE-EYED SAINT.

When Bodhidharma reaches China, the Emperor Wu arrives to welcome him at the entrance of kingdom. Although Bodhidharma by then was a popular Zen patriarch, however, he was known as an ill-tempered, profusely-bearded, wide-eyed saint.

He was referred as "The Blue-Eyed Barbarian".

He, although was welcomed with respect but still people along with the Emperor himself was petrified of his reputation of anger.

The Emperor Wu tried to derive the saint's attention to the Zen temples the kingdom had and the services that were made for the monastic teachings. To all of that Bodhidharma says "Whatsoever" which left the emperor in deep disguise. Bodhidharma continues his journey, however, the Emperor plans to meet him.

On his meeting Bodhidharma asks, what do you have? The Emperor starts thinking and then replies, I have anger.

Bodhidhrama replies, "see me at the temple outside the gate of your palace in the morning". He also asks him to come alone.

The worried Emperor spends the night restless. Reputation, specially an ill one travels very fast and leaves greater impact, so was it about Bodhidharma's anger.

Other day morning, the emperor goes to the temple and Bodhidharma was simply walking. He asked emperor, "Oh you have arrived. Let's go and sit inside". When Emperor Sits then the saint asks, now tell me where the anger is? I will strike it right away with my shaft".

The terrified emperor, thinking that he made a mistake by seeing this crazy man alone, still replies, "How do I know the anger now? It does not come like this."

Bodhidharma says, keep waiting, the moment you find it, let me know I will hit it hard to eliminate your anger.

The Emperor sits and waits, there was no anger. As the Sun rises, he feels light entering inside the temple and through the windowsills, the same light entering in his heart. It was all peace around. Now there was no ego left of Saint ignoring his contribution to the Zen teachings and Monasteries.

Within him he bows down to the saint. It is said

later he requests initiation into monkhood.

The Zen teachings continues. The anger and its food ego both are within us, so is peace and harmony. That's what Emperor Wu takes away that day.


<u>The psychology of anger is dependent. When you try to achieve or attain something and you don't get it, that's where anger starts from. This anger is darkness, the darkness she has seen in herself and being scared of as well. But at times, she met the darkest corners of her own self in those dark moments. She knew it was high time when she required to pull her out of this long time caged person within herself.</u>

# WANDERING

I worship you with a worship that is more than just worship.

I love you with a love that is more than just love...

Away from logics and reasons,

Beyond the madness of adoration,

Farthest from the pinch of expectation,

Above the limits of intimate proximity,

My wandering gave me courage to wander more...find me more.


The journey was long, challenges unlimited. More chances to fail on the way and to lose patience. Shatter down into pieces and stop. What should she choose? What would be the option that she ponders upon?

She knows that she will surely find what she is looking

for.

Where is her search going to end? What were those hidden answers, instead what exactly the questions were?

With every breath, she prayed for the clue and decided to keep her journey on.

# NAGARVADHU TO MONK-FASCINATING JOURNEY OF AMRAPALI.

Amrapali or Ambapali, she was one of the most beautiful woman of the world. The Indian Cleopatra. The first and last woman to de declared as a Nagarvadhu in India history, she was our Ambapali.

From <u>Nagarvadhu to a Monk</u> It is a journey of woman who was celebrated for her extreme beauty, however, that beauty was nothing other than curse for her.

Yet, what a glorious destiny she had.

When? Since her early teenage, this girl was already popular for her extraordinary charm and appearance in and around Vaishali democracy of Ancient India.

There is no much to mention about childhood of Amrapali, however, very interesting reason behind her name. No one knows of her mother, she was spontaneously born in the foot of mango tree, hence she was named as a combination of Sanskrit words Amra that means Mango and Pallav, the young leaves. On the other hand, the feudal lord Mahanama, Amrapali was said to be born to him. He was so enchanted by his child's exceptional beauty that he left the kingdom and moved to a small village in Vaishali.

Unaware of what was coming to her in future, the girl happily enjoyed her childhood with her feudal parents. But the charm and grace of this innocent child grew faster than her.

Everyone who saw her, desired her. Wanted an ownership over her. This had become a bigger problem for her feudal father. The Nobel men, kings, feudal lords and the situation was such that if decided for one, the others would have created massacre.

To mention that probably for the first time the parliament of state of Vaishali had to intervene to decide on the ownership of Amrapali and after long discussion that continued for days, the parliament announced this epitome of grace as a Nagarvadhu, a prostitute, no one owned her, she was served to all. Although she could choose her companion but could not be committed to one.

The question is, was not it easy to ask Amrapali

herself and let her decide her future instead the whole state owning her?

Prostitution, those days was not about objectifying sex. It was more of artistry. Singing, dancing and serving that would ease worries of a man visiting her. Thankfully, persuading for physical intimacy, without willingness of the woman was not considered as an act of pride.

Amrapali's fame added to the fame of the democracy of Vaishali which in course of time brought attacks as well over the state by King Bimbisara of Magadh kingdom.

For Amrapali, this was all her life. It is quite possible that she was unaware of the other aspects of life as since she could understand, what she always observed was a fight over her ownership and then it ended making her a bride of whole State.

However, destiny had another story for her. On Buddha's visit to Vaishali, it so happened that Amrapali attended a sermon near mango grove which she had developed. The sermon by Buddha moved her and she invited Buddha along with his bhikhus to her grove. There she had an opportunity to serve food to Buddha.

All his bhikhus were surprised to know Buddha accepting her invitation with silence. They also were worried that this was possibly going to defame

Buddha. Buddha rejected all other invitations from feudal lords and kings around.

To his disciples, on their confusion, Buddha says, let's see who is deeper in our karmas? He knew, whosoever is, will persuade the other.

May be he was aware that this persuasion would again be something already ordained.

Buddha visits her royal grove and then the destiny unfolds, she could feel the realm of actual way of living of a human. Amrapali asks for ordinance. Initiation to monkhood.

Amrapali, the nagarvadhu henceforth was remembered as a Buddhist monk who gave away all her futile belongings to Buddhahood.

From Courtesan, a rajya nartaki to monkhood, she served in true sense.

Was this transformation of Ambapali of one incident, one day? No, it was her journey. The quest might have always been there. It was just that she was not paying an attention to her own inner calling. One day she had an opportunity that gave her power to see through the clouds. Amrapali was really fortunate so as she did not have to wander much. She opened her eyes and saw the sun shine.

There are many who wander and keep yearning. They are sensitive towards their unease but the answers are still not clear.

Like her yearning, her wandering also continues. She is growing as a wanderer, travelling deep into the dense fog. Moment to moment the blanket of fog thickened, yet she kept on walking. Unsure that the turns she took in the journey were leading to the destination or not, yet she kept on taking the risk. What was this risk about? Taking the wrong path or getting lost in it. Wandering is scary as it brings uncertainty.

But the point is, unless you reach the destination, no one knows the righteousness of the path. Here, in this journey even the destination is unknown as of now. However, stopping never looked like an option to her. Technically, it is not for anyone. There is another way to look at wandering. It brings hopes too. You keep walking with an expectation to find that unknown pleasure that could be your ultimate nest.

She chose former option with grace. Wandering to find the lost horizon.

++++++++++++++++++++++++++++++++++++++++++++++++++++++++++++++++++++++++

She was joyous, she was thrilled, although a little frightened too. She just wanted to see the other side when the birds would start chirping melody and the bright ray will make its way through opaque and reach her. She just strives, she just waits and she believes that the answers are hidden. She feels the aroma of her tranquiliser, which she has been diving in since childhood.

Why was she here? What was the purpose of her being? She finds the density growing. She feels as if she is drowning into the dark tranquillity. She recognized this situation. It had happened time and again she finds herself close to her answers, but she slips back again and reaches to some new stony alley.

****************************************************

If she is in search of something, what is that? She was feeling an urge to paint a canvas, she picks up the brush and tries to select a shade to start with and she felt confused about the shade. Now again the question rises, if she is to decide on one single shade, why is there so much of self-struggle required? Who was this, who was always sitting inside to throw another suggestion, to question the first choice she made? She had read it somewhere that the mind plays games with us. Where does this mind come from? Where it otherwise remained? Why was it so prominent as soon as she made a choice in life? As soon as she decided what to do with her life, she always heard a voice standing against her, which emerged from somewhere unknown. May be if she made a choice just to survive, this another person could have stood against that too. Thankfully, it was not to be decided by her.

She wanted to find this another person living in her body. This person kept on creating lots of chaos in her otherwise settled self.

She dropped the idea and started reading a book. It was a holiday, she had basically nothing to do. Even book could not help her to distract from her thoughts about mind. She called one of a friend and they planned to meet. As decided, they met at the coffee shop which was convenient for both of them to reach.

Unfortunately, she could not enjoy the coffee, neither the conversation. Again the mind starts, questions happen, what was the reason to leave house? Who wanted to meet the friend? Why was not she feeling happy in the presence of her friend? Surprisingly they were known to each other for long.

After some time, she asks her friend for a movie, which she denied suggesting that they should sit and talk for some time for her friend, had already noticed the anxiety building in her.

After asking repetitively, she tried to share, although in the process she busted into tears and at that moment, when she let herself be free, she realised how much she had stored. She was tired of the confusion so much that she needed to talk about it. She shared with her friend and after that, she asked that whether it was alright?

This was a beautiful suggestion by her friend, and she asked her to understand what was she upset of? Whether of this another person, or this person being questioning her thoughts. What was the main purpose of her trying to find this person or the mind, whatever she understood it to be? They hugged each other and left with a commitment to meet again next weekend at her house.

Next day she went at work, completely unhappy as now she had been given another task, which was again questioning her.

Two days had gone, clueless. She did not have any answer to share with her friend. On the third day, she was walking down the lane to reach home, she was crossing through an ice cream shop, on the wall, was a quotation written that caught her attention and she entered into the shop. The quote was "What you are seeking for is within you".  She ordered a scoop of cream and crust and sat reading the quote again and again. What she could see now, the mind or the other person she thought lives in her body was she. She, who was firming her own search; her own wandering. Her inner voice, that was helping her to understand that the supreme power that she was trying to find outside somewhere, was inside her only.

The day arrived when she was supposed to meet her friend. She happily welcomed her in with a broad smile on her face. She thanked her friend for forcing her to pay attention to the voice that was emerging from within her. She shared as this quest of her had already grown inside very deep to believe that there was a separate super power guiding her and this entire universe. She could never realize that the power was in her, with her. She then shared that there have been incidences how this inner self had played games, yet helped her to take better decisions and make better choices.

Today, she was ready to complete her painting.

<u>**"What you hear, is your own pure voice; your own voice gives you courage to find your answers."**</u>

The one who we are looking for outside, is already in us. He, who completes the cycle with us and he who plans our life with us, is the one who is within us and whose presence is felt everywhere and every time.

# DENY ME NOT YOUR ETERNAL BEAUTY- RABIA BASRI

Everyone like crazy were looking for the lost needle. Maybe whole village had gathered to find that small particle as it was Rabia's. Yes Rabia Basri, one of the few female sufi mystics. By then she probably was not even saint but people loved her and respected her mysticism.

Everyone wanted to find that needle for her, to help her. After hours, no one could. Of course finding a needle on the pathway, a road was not easy. And gradually it had started to darken outside. Villagers started getting tired and worried equally as in sometime it was going to be completely dark, night, the silent, serene but dark. Along with that it was getting cold too. Rabia gets a lamp from inside and motivates everyone to keep finding the lost needle.

Finally one of the villagers asks Rabia whether she remembers where she exactly dropped it.   Her answer leaves everyone stunned and furious too.

She says, she lost the needle inside her room. Villagers now were furious and they asked when the needle was lost inside, why she made them all search for it outside, in the cold evening, in the dark, when of course there was no chance of finding.

On that Rabia replies, "But that is what you all are doing since ages."

"O Lord, if I worship you because of Fear of Hell,

then burn me in Hell,

If I worship you because I desire Paradise,

then exclude me from Paradise.

But if I worship you for yourself alone,

then deny me not your Eternal Beauty- Rabia Basri

Rabia's life was totally devoted to love of God, the ascetic life and self-denial

More than her absolute asceticism, is the concept of Divine Love that Rabia introduced. She was the first to introduce the idea that God should be loved for God's own sake. There is another very important incident of this Sufi Mystic's life.

On her way she often came across a man crying outside the mosque. One day while she was crossing, this man was furious and angry, he was yelling at lord saying for how long is he going to wait outside? Why is not he able to get in? Why is not the door opening for him? That was the day of his realization.

That very moment Rabia, who was passing by, stood near this almost insane man and told him, the door is open, what are you waiting for. This man was Hassan -Al- Basri, another popular Sufi mystic.

What Rabia said that day to Hassan is still not understood and accepted by many. Those who have, could drop the struggle with themselves. They stopped finding, because they realized that the seeker and the seeking are same.

It was never, and it is never that the door of a temple or a mosque is supposed to open. It is the door within ourselves which needs a push.

Today she feels that the confusion, the seeker, the finding and the way is all within her. The noise, the voice and the chaos, all are from within. It's her inner voice that sometimes finds Red colour interesting and sometimes her favourite shade, she feels is orange.

Now the pure inner voice was going to give her the answers, yet it is not still easy.

# OH MY BELOVED!!!

You entered my heart, through the glance of eyes,

Who knew I was yet to experience ties,

You evoked my senses,

I felt traveling through tenses

I felt the rush of emotions,

My heart screamed in passion,

I saw myself flowing directionless,

I was actually growing relentless.

Like the high tide waves, I was passing through the caves.

Was about to reach the light, however, was thrown aside.

I know I am empty actually, however I take it gracefully.

To it there are reasons, which won't change like seasons.

You gave me memories to cherish. I saw the sorrow vanish.

You give me reasons to smile. The one that helps me walk miles.

How do I tell you my beloved? In you I saw HIM.

Your glimpse connects me to the one supreme...

You are unaware of the reality...

In the stolen gazes you gave me the pleasure to eternity.

Knock, Knock!!! There was some noise on the door, while she was sitting into deep serene state, she heard something. She opened the door. There was a cool breeze that caressed her cheek, she felt scent of wet mud in her nostrils. She tried to open her eyes, but could not. "Let me live in this beautiful reverie", said her heart. She could not understand what the reason of this unexpected pleasure inside her was. She again tried to open her eyes to have a glance of the composure she felt in that moment. It was something new, something that she had never come across. She was on top of the world. She wanted to dance, and she did too. She wanted to sing the song that her heart created, and she did. Each and every word that aroused from her heart went back to her, deeper somewhere. She felt she could fly, as if she had wings of her own. Sky seemed to be in her reach, she jumped and almost touched, however she fell down. What happens next? She holds a hand. She feels a firm grip of warmth around her. The energy pulls her towards the source. She stands straight and tries to look into the eyes of this energy. Those deep eyes looked to be the window that could take her right to her own soul. She peeped in them and felt as if she saw her entire life in the fraction of seconds. She could see herself moment to moment crossing the timelines. This energy now felt to be familiar. Once again she was soaked in the questions. What was this energy? Why did she feel safe and calm in its presence? How could she see herself in it? Why did she feel that she could fly like a free bird in the sky? Why did she feel the strength to touch the horizon? Although she could not.

She wanted to touch it and feel its form while her eyes were closed. It seemed to have a shape and form of a human. She started moving her hands caressing that warmth of affection that she felt in that silence. She felt a magnetic association with it. She tried to go away, however she was pulled back towards him. Who was HE? She once again gathered all the verve and opened her eyes. What she could see was Light. A circle of light, shining so bright that she had to close her eyes again. It was again magic, how come was it possible that despite of the utter illumination, his eyes were so peaceful. So clear that she could read his heart from his eyes in a twinkling of a star. She found two hearts talking, knitting a beautiful bond of emotions together. She heard herself saying that she was for him in this world, to which he reciprocates by holding her hand softly. The gentle touch, however, firm enough to ensure her that she had reached to her safe haven. What more she would ask for, all her yearnings vanished. She had been sailing into the ocean for ages, purposeless. As if, for a lifetime and the tides kept throwing her from one longing to another and her yearning kept deepening. She finally had reached to the shore, the place where she could sit and relax.

She thought of resting in HIS arms, she kept her head on his shoulder and dozed off. She then sees that a pretty girl in a pink colour frock was standing cuddling her white teddy in her arms. It looked as if she loved her teddy very much. She patted it, talked to it, and shared her emotions with it. May be it was an inseparable part of her. She looked very happy holding it in her arms, so proud to have it with her. Far away she sees horizon, as if the sky was leaning down to plant a kiss to the Earth, and earth stretching her arms to hold the sky forever. This little girl with teddy wanted to touch the sky. She starts running with her favourite article in her hand. She keeps on running, trying to touch the sky. She takes a leap, the distance moves farther, she runs again, panting breath, aching legs, holding her teddy tight, she keeps on running. She was about to give up but what she sees is a beautiful orange line in the sky, as if sun was to set in the lap of mother earth. She was joyful to see that serenity, more excited to have a close view of it, she collects herself, holding her teddy tighter, runs again. Her tired self, still grooving in excitement, she again takes a leap...but what ?....she loses balance and falls. She has tears rolling down her cheeks, not due to the pain that happened as she got hurt on her knees...the tears rolled because she dropped her adorable bundle of happiness, her teddy. She might have dropped it, when she fell but she could not find it. She stood back again, although broken, tried for another leap as she found the sky closer, a curve of redness that resembled of a smile on a toddlers face appeared all over the sky...she jumps.

She finds herself in the middle of ocean again... fighting with tides... trying to find a direction. She tries to recall how she had reached to the ocean, she could not think of anything other than relaxing on the shore with HIM. Whom, she thought to be her sustenance. She thought HIM to be her destination. Where was he? Her heart had sunk for once, thinking of his wellbeing. She tried to recall HIS face, but realised she never saw him.

She had only felt HIS presence around her. The comforting energy flowing from HIM weaving a layer of strength and confidence around her heart. HIS fragrance was all that she could remember about HIM. For once she felt lifeless. She wanted to scream and shout. Who was there to listen to her painful screams?? She cries her heart out, feels the pain of thousand bruises.

# BLUE ORCHIDS

To you my beloved,

I have to say,

there were blue orchids blooming.

On the neckline you touched,

I turn towards right,

bow down a little,

 And take the fragrance of those tiny creatures you implanted.

They were alive enough to give me life...

Now as it is long that they had their life,

they are turning pale,

The blue orchids that lived by your touch,

have started to shrivel.

Watering them with two droplets from my eyes...

I keep them alive to offer them to your feet,
when you be back
To take my orchids to the place where they never fade.
In my Perseverance, is always you,
keeping me with my orchids alive.

# MAJNUN-AN HONOUR

Who was the receiver of this honour? The mad crazy lover Qays, the one who was completely possessed by the love of Laila. Drunken the nectar of immortal belongingness.

This story is Arabic, however, later popularized by many poets and mystics in various languages and versus, adding their own understanding of this serenity of love.

Somewhere we come across versus that Qays was so much captivated by Laila that he started to mention her in his poetries. He shouted her name often and people called him crazy. Since then Qays becomes Majnun.

It is said that Majnun went with the marriage proposal to Laila's father to which he rejected looking at Majnun's insane behaviour.

Laila was later married to a rich, good looking merchant of Arab.

On knowing that, Majnun leaves behind his home and walks with the marriage procession continuously shouting for Laila.

Looking at the madness of this man would have defamed Laila, hence, the mad poor lover was pelted by stones. Quite possible, since then there is a trend to hit stones to the mad or the lover.

However, possibly those people there were unaware of Majnun's richness that he was absorbed already by his love Laila. Some say Laila too was so much in love with Majnun that she could not survive the separation and died early.

Mujnun on the other hand was already dead. He kept on wandering calling out Laila, chanting his poetries that he created for his love.

All the poetries were popularised later in Turkish and Persian languages. The Persian poet Baba Taher mentions the love between Laila and Majnun in his poetries.

The story of Laila and Majnun happened to be one of the most popular ones in India lately.

Annihilation is the appropriate term that Majnun taught to the world, but here there is a catch. This Annihilation was not finishing yourself in love. This Annihilation was about being one with the love. Or to put it correctly, finding love within yourself. One's own state of being. They were two flesh one soul, hence later the two between them vanished and they became Laila Majnun.

On discovering about the death of Laila, Majnun wandering took a different form. Crossing the desert, between storm he falls down, there was a source of water, it was years since Majnun had drank water or eaten a morsel.

That day, he saw himself on the surface of water, but what he actually saw was Laila. He saw Laila instead of his face. The moment that might have been the freedom and liberation for Majnun.

Driven mad by Laila, drunken in Laila, he finds Laila within himself.

Once someone asks Majnun…

Oh Majnun, the lord, the Allah is calling you, on which Majnun replies, Oh silly man, 'why am I supposed to go to Allah? Tell him, if he wants to see, he can come to me as Laila'.

When the god calls the crazy lover for merger, the craziest love shouts out, for beloved, instead of God for the love knows that if solace is somewhere it is in the love. This love is the supreme power, for love itself is the lord that resides within, just the way Majnun finds his Laila within him. But, the challenge is surrender and acceptance is not easy.

**Majnun could, so did Nanak, although in a different way. that's why they could submerge in their beloved.**

---

This is who the beloved she is going to find now. The one, whom she lost in that ocean, that shapeless beloved was within her. His fragrance was always to remain in her. She just needs to find him, within her.

Now why would she require anyone to hear her painful screams as her beloved was with her always. Why would she scream only? She will find HIM in her, beneath the layers of her own identity. May her love survive till the time of her annihilation?

Drowned in love be Fanaa in self.

# FANAA

Walking barefoot on the bed of plush green grass, she feels tickled, she closes her eyes and giggle.

Keeping the eyes closed, she continues to walk..

The soft bed is replaced with a hot iron plate.

A tadpole comes hoping to her, pulls the loose end of her drape,

She gives him her ears, and he yells saying

"Will you now open your eyes?'

Your feet has burns and boils.

She tries to pat him, however, by now the tadpole has become a butterfly,

So, it flies.

Her eyes are still closed,

As she is holding her beloved in them, the one she lost

near the ocean.

Hence, she refuses to open, how come would she let him go again?

Walking with the boils, she achieves ecstasy, as holding the love is holding your own soul.

You don't love by soul, to the soul…Love is soul.

In complete surrender to self, you find the extreme pleasure within self.

Sipping a glass of fresh lime in the office cafeteria she was thinking, is love truly so important for survival. Is that what she misses in life? The love and affection she feels lost once she was a child, is it that which haunts her? Is it that what has created this vacuum in her life?

Love is not a form, it is an emotion and most importantly the state. She tries to understand that from the story of Laila-Majnun. It is not something between opposite genders, a man and a woman. Thinking of love, she feels it is something beyond biological specification. Above the transaction of touch and feel like emotions. It is about nourishment of soul. A connection beyond time and age, beyond lifetime.

This nourishment starts from the lap of mother and grows until you find it within yourself, however, the prime fact is love is existence. All others are just forms.

# THE YEARNING!!!

The yearning continues...

I yearn for the tight hug,

I yearn for a long sleep,

I yearn to be caressed,

I yearn not to be judged and assessed.

I yearn to have back that lost piece of my peace,

I yearn for that moment that makes the storm inside freeze.

I yearn for the smile that spreads without a pinch of pain,

I yearn for the preposition that has no loss or gain.

May be I am broken, maybe I will lose...

To find my way and to write my say, is the all what I choose

I keep my hopes alive till my yearning continues.

# AFFECTION-LOVE OF EXISTENCE, BY EXISTENCE FOR EXISTENCE

The moment when her heart sinks, she hides herself in her lap. Rolling down her cheeks, a drop of that tiny tear falls on her lip. The salty taste shakes her and she feel that contend that has been going on and on. She slips into the flashback and remembers the journey till now. The days when she was just a child, too small to even recognize the pain, she still could manage to get over whatever came across. She held her own hands while crossing the road to reach to her school. Solved the decimals on her own, danced on the music she created in her mind and kissed herself when her teacher made stars on her notebook. She tore the pages from her book, if she could not solve the word problems, but kept them safe to get the appropriate solution one day. She befriended herself when alone and unfriended those who told her she was good for none. She braided her hair on her own and patted herself to sleep.

But she still misses the fragrance of curry leaves and asafoetida that her mother used as tadka for dal.

The journey had not been easy; however, still she is on her way. She has decided that she is not going to stop for being unsure. She will not close her eyes even if it is dark around. She will walk into the darkness with her eyes wide open till the time she reaches to the other side of the tunnel that shows ray of light, ray of hope.

---

What exactly is it? An energy for the sustenance of the humanity as a whole.

If we try to find out, we may never have one specific logic that can define love for love itself is not logical. It does not analyze, does not evaluate, and does not comprehend.

It just flows. Creates a chain, connects all of us together.

What is love or affection? Maybe an emotion, maybe a feeling driven by external reasons?

Love-Accepting in totality.

However, it this acceptance in totality possible? The basic trait two people share is always love. As love only is a state of being of a human.

Yes, in the journey, we happen to wrap ourselves with so many outwardly layers that this basic phenomena-Love is hidden.

**<u>Probably that's what her mother did at that point of time. Probably, now she is doing the same.</u>**

Mother starts loving the child the moment she feels another one heart beating in her womb, it's divine. With that love, she nourishes the child inside her and once her bundle of abundance is in her arms, the love flourishes the child. Right from the beginning Love is a necessity. Have we seen a mother loving her two different children differently? Does she love a child of her partially and another one completely? Does her love vary based on the skills, traits, and looks of the child?

We do not come across such a situation.

What is the reason behind this? Love is her state of being. As a mother, she is filled with compassion for her children. Now it does not matter to her whether her one child excels in academics and other does not. Yes, she puts in extra effort, now that's a totally different area of discussion so let's not indulge into its correctness, however, her that extra effort too, is an outcome of love.

Similarly, for anyone and at any stage of life, the basic emotion of love is always our own state of being. We can love our partner or spouse, only in case we are able to in the first place. If we are compassionate for animals, if we feel happiness looking at a blooming flower, if drizzling makes us dance, that's the strength of love that we have within us.

If we lack that state, all the bonds that we establish in a lifetime are going to end up as a relationship of convenience, then they will depend on actions, behavior, and circumstances of life.

As we spoke about drizzling and rains, the love is such emotion, such a state that it gives you the strength to accept the slurry sludge as well along with the fragrance of wet soil.

Love stops you from judgments.

Let us all find our state of being, maybe we will have more clarity about ourselves. Maybe we will stop suffocating each other by adding unnecessary expectations and obligations. Love yourself and be love. Love is all around. It is the only way of living. Love only can nurture one's being as it is not the relationship or a bond. It is simply a state of being of an individual.

Life does not treat us all in the same way. Born as a tiny bundle of joy she brought the moments of extreme happiness for her family. Her tiny, bright eyes could notice the cheer and glee in every eye. They held her, cherished her, with affection. Fed her with compassion. Pair of hands was always ready to comfort her whenever she cried. She felt comfortable wrapped with the arms full of love. It was a divine feeling. That was her small world. She started growing up with all the luxury one could think of. She started babbling and crawling. Few hearts went out in glee when she took her first step individually.

However, what was it, that went erroneous in the journey? Suddenly those comforting and compassionate hands were replaced by so much of anger. Love was something she craved for since then. She saw pity, she found misery, she even offered prayers for that, but all that was useless, for she kept on craving for the lap to put her head in, the pat on her back when she excelled in academics, pride in those pairs of eyes when she held the trophy in hands. Yes, she saw some moisture in eyes, whenever she expected a large smile. She was not enough mature then to understand those tears were also an outcome of hidden love which could not flourish much to provide the extreme confidence in her.

"The cycle of life, the stages between first breaths to last breath combined together is the gist of the presence of that one supreme power. He, the one who does not appear in form, cannot be seen by our virtual eyes, but in moments of utter silence, you see the glimpses. Every breath we take is an affirmation of HIS presence. We live in an illusion of taking control of things, of directing our lives; however, ultimately you realize that you were merely a puppet. Yes, a puppet but the favourite one. HE keeps the strings in his control and watches you perform the task he assigns you. HE sees you fall, HE sees you rise, watches you making mistakes and with them becoming wise. HE is always with you, in you. Opening ways and guiding through the correct one. But you need to walk, and keep the faith that he will make you do so."

---

She wakes up in the middle of the night, sweating and furious. This was too much to digest and believe. We are puppets, or were living being, we breathe, we respond, we feel and we love. How was it to be believed that we were nothing? How can we have strings attached to us in someone else's control?

She has always found herself angry due to few blockages that she is unable to fight through. There are days now when she feels that she is burdened of holding it all so tight and close to her heart that no one is allowed to enter to that corner. In fact, she also ignores, but not completely, for to ignore also she needs to face the truth of her life again and again.

She again goes back to the teddy that she drops while running to touch the horizon. That soft toy was very dear to her. She starts assuming, when it dropped, why did not she go back and try to find her? She kept on running towards horizon. What did she have in the end, lost horizon as well as lost piece of her heart?

She starts thinking that it was a lifeless thing, what if it had a life. Now she shivers, what comes in front of her is that girl, in pink frock. Now she sees the girl dropped, rashes and blood all over, lot of pain in her body.

It was the situation she in few years back. She had felt that touch many a times which she did not know was a bad touch. That day, was an end to it, however, an end to her as well. That girl in pink frock was rushed to the hospital by her parents. By the time she was back to senses, they were discussing one word again and again, poor girl. It was something that she heard for the first time. Of course she was just a child to know, why suddenly had she turned into a poor child, subject of pity. Unfortunately she had to as after that incident, the life changed so much that she still feels the heat around.

She was irate due to the situation, but more than on anything or anyone, with herself. She did not allow herself to have friends. She does not believe in people. She did not even believe in that super natural power. Maybe she thought that if there was any power, why at the first place she had to go through all of it at that tender age. She lost her love for relatives and something was very serious as after that she never saw her mother smiling or caressing her the way she did earlier. Her anger ablaze more.

She is now aware that this is a dirt behind many doors and unfortunately, we ourselves close them and choose to punish ourselves instead of the one who deserves. However, the bigger trouble is that we probably never overcome. Live in anger, guilt and disappointment. Acceptance is probably much required in order to liberate our own selves and then probably forgiving will happen.

This forgiveness is more required again for oneself not for the other. To be able to live in totality, in the present moment, it is important to unload the burden of past, which continuously is adding to anger within us.

Now the problem is that anger was making her more vulnerable.

The hatred she had in her was taking toll.

Although, she knew that she needs to be free of this. She needs to overcome the anger, the hatred but past always remained in present and kept on hampering the future preceding.

As per the Greek Story, there lived two brothers, the sons of Titan. The Titan who fought against Zeus and due to which the Titan was chained and sent to the lower world.

Unlike the other humans, his sons were not like other men nor like God. Name of the elder brother was Prometheus and younger one was called Epimetheus.

They both had special characters Prometheus was one who always thought of coming days, future, may be day ahead, a year or a decade. All his actions were future oriented. He was always busy planning to make world wiser and better. But that was for forthcoming days or years.

He went out to live with humans to plan for their better future. He taught them to save themselves with the help of fire, they learnt to cook food and lit their caves. He made them believe that 'A new golden Age shall come, brighter and better by far than the old'.

The story says that Prometheus, seeing the people dying of cold and being eaten by beasts in the dark nights, he goes to Zeus, the Greek God to ask for some fire, to which he denies.

As he was a fore thinker, he knew fire will save the humankind. He found stalk of fennel on his way back and when he broke it, he found it hollow. He lit it to find that it could stay light. Then he stole fire from volcano to light it.

Now what this teaches is even hollowness is useful and may bring brightness to the darker thoughts.

However, later in this story what we get to see is even the fore thinker Prometheus was chained by Zeus for his actions. Epimetheus was already lost in past but then enters Hercules, one who freed Prometheus from the chains. Hercules, the son of God Zeus again was chained and bounded in his own misconceptions completely forgotten about his super powers.

During his imprisonment, his mother Hera meets him and reminds him of the supernatural powers Hercules had. He had acquired them of the divine milk from his mother's breast. That was the moment when Hercules was in complete present, in total surrender that he could realise his powers and saved Prometheus and the world later.

So ultimate realization is in the power of present. Living in present moment as the future may someday come to life, past is already gone. The day when future comes to life that say it will be the present day. So probably there is no future as such and at the same time no relevance of past.

Both the Prometheus and Epimetheus live within us, but the day we realize the Hercules in us, we are liberated from the trap of this past and future. For past is gone, future never comes.

She would one day realize her powers when she starts acknowledging her present, leaving the past back and future aside. Till then her wandering and her journey has to continue.

# S-'HE'

Woman is a creator. She has a capacity to create something within her. She nurtures, she feeds she cares for everyone. Womanhood is to be celebrated, to be worshipped. Why a woman has to face heinous acts against the strongest quality she has in her? She is compassionate, loving, caring and fragile. This fragility is considered as her weakness often. That weakness, although is her strength.

Her thorax holds her identity. She carries her baby in her womb, and once the child is born, only a woman is capable of breast feeding. Of course, it is a biological fact, however the facts are also for a reason. Only a woman can be so selfless when it comes to sharing. We remember here an incident from Sati Anusuiya's life. The way she decided to feed the tridev is phenomenal keeping her dignity she fulfills their request. She has her attention on it.

Having spoken about motherhood, she remembers her domestic help. She at times brings her children when she comes for work. Generally on Sundays and holidays. She has a daughter and a son. She observes the girl, little girl, she keeps on trying to help her mother beyond her capacities.

Is not that exactly what motherhood is? Selflessness and patience. Do one really needs to give birth to be a mother?

Is not motherhood also about emotion? There could be a possibility that a man has motherhood in him. It is about the state of being instead of few body parts.

She is now wondering, if this universal idea is understood, would not it help people to be more compassionate towards each other. Maybe the difference of gender and genitals would not matter gradually.

# DEALING WITH THE STORAGE-JUDGEMENT

The perfection- The self-imposed expectation.

She got agitated with the smallest of reasons. Maybe due to additional ounce of sugar in her cup of coffee. Speed of fan that was not as per her comfort, spill of water the minor things was enough to make her furious.

Angry inside her, she faces lots of trouble every day.

She does not exactly know, who is she angry with?

What was this anger for? She knew that everything that happened in triggered one emotion commonly. That was anger. Expressed or not it was always there.

What happened every time, whenever she was angry? She hurt herself the most. She worked extra hours as she wanted to avoid unnecessary clash and arguments, she worked on behalf of all her subordinates.

She remembers how a small mistake in a Slideshow prepared by one of her subordinate made her mad. However, above all was how badly she cursed herself for not being watchful, whereas it was just a simple miss of glance. One minor thing that was overlooked by her, even if it was major, was it a question of life and death? Is not it fine to make mistakes. Human errors, what we call. The term might not have existed if the error was a crime never to be committed.

Why these soaring expectations with self? Why judging and tagging yourself? These questions she always had, but could not find the reason.

After these bouts of anger subsided, she sat with herself to think what was the solution to these anger episodes?

She knew that was not doing right with herself. Ultimately the question is, what was this anger?

It was a by-product of the journey and various episodes of life. Maybe the lost horizon, the dense fog, the lost teddy or the broken self.

Yes, now there was a change though, hopefully it stays in her. She has encountered the softer and purer self at the ocean shore.

# ECSTASY-FREEDOM AND LIBERATION

Talking of Ecstasy, it is a vague term. Ecstasy is a different phenomenon.

When your heart is bursting in those silent moments; tears starts flowing from your eyes, and there is ecstasy.

You have been weaker when you tried redirecting your emotion, now it is your strength

Transition of madness to sanity. Artificial-ism to original-ism

Rejoice, dance, clap, sing and similarly do not prevent yourself from flowing. It is the cleansing that is much required.

Celebration of self-acceptance.

She although wants an escape from her anger and self-pity, yet she has by now understood that it was not possible as she tried her best. She knew that there was no other way of liberation than to accept all your emotions, accept yourself. This acceptance of self could only open the way of acceptance for all. To accept, of course it was very important to know the self. So now she knew that all the strength and weakness came from within. There was no outer source that if you could turn down would stop troubling you. Gradually the questions were fading.

It is actually what you see outside is a result of you as inside.

Looking for love she found God and looking for God, she found self. The search that was outward, changed the way and took turn inside.

Still Questions remain, the ones which were merely because of the feeling of self-pity, Why me? Why always me?

# LIFE: AN UNRESOLVED MYSTERY.

Life that is said to be a biological process of physical entities. Yet there is no proper definition of life. Is breathing life? Or is life anything that eventually grows and dies? Or may be a self-organising chemistry encoded in DNA.

Neither scientists nor philosophers, no one could really describe life.

We see it through whichever is the closer prospect for us.

Now as there is nothing clear, can we call life, an aimless expedition?

The moment, we call it aimless, the problem begins, now we all start finding aim for the life as it is very difficult to enjoy the bliss without purpose. Just living, that is impossible.

Finding meaning and purpose of life that is the opportunity we are bestowed with.

In simple words, life is an opportunity to create meaning. To attain it, we just have to live it. However, we misunderstand the life and try imposing so much to it that we lose the real essence of life.

The body was laying on the floor, wrapped in white piece of cloth. This cloth looked like a shroud. The body pale and lifeless. But why was it placed outside of the house, Inside there was a beautiful little world. She had developed it giving up her peace of mind, her strength, and her emotions all to this one place that she thought she would live forever in.

This beautiful abode was a witness to her struggles, the pains and moments of happiness were grander inside the beautiful walls of this house. Oh walls, she remembers how much brainstorming had happened just to choose the colour of one wall.

However those times of quarrel and arguments were also the part of pleasure as they brought lots of satisfaction. A beautiful family that lived together inside this adobe, for all of them each and every detail mattered a lot.

A shade of curtain, a size of couch, every minute detail was so important.

She was not liking this white cloth she was wrapped in, she has cupboards full of beautiful attires for all occasions. She loved all the colours, however this shroud was not a happy thing.

Why was so much of rush there, around this body. People, all of them seemed to be talking about it. Few looked genuinely concerned, few were there just for a formality, yet the good thing was they were there. Few faces, she could not even recognize, wondering who were they, she starts recollecting the memories of life time.

The mother's womb is safest place always, yet you can live there only for a specific time, you are bond to see the world and face it all by yourself.

The journey called life, is different for each one of us, however, one thing remains as a universal fact that the journey is going to happen, you wish for it or not. You will walk the roads that are decided for you. There is no escape, and you are going to walk alone those unknown trails. Directionless, flow you may find, however, for sure whatever you come across, is certain to have. Now no one knows who ascertains your journey, who plans your ways, in fact at times, you may think as if you were making choices, and taking decisions, however, today it seems clear that it is not us, who plan the journey.

Although, the body lying was pale and lifeless, but the face held serenity and calm. May be a satisfaction of completing one circle of life. May be a result of expectation that she was finally reaching where we are meant to be.

At times she saw a smile on the face of the dead. What made this smile appear? The memories of the life time, the role she played as a finest actor or did she have a glimpse of astral world? May be the body was now waiting for the transition to happen. She sitting at the corner could she the preview of the world that was pure.

Oh!! There was some noise, the mortuary van has arrived. All the dear ones came closer to the body lying, to lift it and place in there, and the end of journey starts for the new beginning.

Why did they leave her? She had to go with her, just to see now what was next for this body.  But she was left behind.

**<u>The only truth of life is death. The end of a journey, or a real beginning?</u>**

**<u>Respect life, there is nothing as holy as it.</u>**

Now, heard many times, yet a works as a reminder

A very popular story -Just a visitor

Once a person was in search of true lesson. He got to know of a Sufi saint and he planned to visit him to learn important lessons for life.

He starts his journey to the saint, there was no proper road to the hut. He travelled through the dirt and dust, surrounded by the Jungle.

He was much fascinated as he had heard a lot about the Sufi saint in the vicinity of town. He anyways wanted to meet him so he continues the journey and finally reaches to the hut of saint.

On his arrival, he finds the saint working silently.

He introduces himself and shares his purpose of visit.

Saint offers him a cup of tea. The visitor was silently sipping his tea, the saint continued to work as he was earlier.

But there was a difference in the silence of both of them. The Saint knew the question and visitor was hesitating to ask.

Saint knew he was observing something which was very important for him.

Finally the Saint stops and makes him comfortable by saying, "tell me what you want to know?'

The visitor then replies, "I have been observing, your hut

is empty?" He was astonished to see that the Sufi's home was a very simple room. The only furniture was a mat and a kerosene lamp. Floor was clean and swept with mud.

To that the saint replies, "What do you expect me to have?"

The visitor says, "You have no furniture".

Saint answers, "So don't you"

'But I am just a visitor', replies the visitor, hesitating

And Saint's reply on that mesmerizes him, the saint says, "So am I, since ages".

The visitor bows down to the master on receiving the lesson for lifetime.

# THE QUANTUM LEAP

Revolving in the radius of his presence,

Saw his glimpse through his eyes,

Flute played a soulful rhythm,

And I felt my breath merging with supreme,

Only this 'I', divided me from him,

Now this amalgamation makes us single entity,

For a moment the reverie sparkled,

Life flowed from this to that world,

We took the leap in quantum,

Kissing the divine sanctity,

Dissolved in purity,

Insane nomads, after lives of roving

We were vanished in us,

One world, one soul, one breath,
And the rhythm stops,
Flute lost.

Now wherever you see, you find him, you find yourself.

Once Guru Nanak Devji was travelling to the pilgrimage, the holy Mecca to the stone of Kabba with Muslim devotees. Once reaching there, it was evening he planned to rest a little and fell asleep fast. While sleeping his feet were towards the Kabba. The devotees come and wake him up asking to change his direction. On that Nanak smiles and asks, so give me one direction where HE is not present.

---

The beloved she lost in dreams in the ocean, the affectionate mother, the happiness and dignity, the girl in pink frock, the teddy and the lost horizon, all were suddenly back in her arms. She could visualize them. See them all around. Just one realisation.

The introspection that she could have with self was the most beautiful experience.

She was now peaceful for she knew that happiness, satisfaction and success was the result of what we already have within ourselves.

Where the opportunity to introspect does comes from?

That too comes from within. Why do we have different taste for colour and music? Just the same way, we have different journey.

Ramana Maharshi escaped his home when he was just seventeen. There are lots of people who are his disciples today. People worship him, visit Ramana Ashram religiously. Maharshi's teachings are very simple. He teaches just to live.

He did escape out of fear. The fear of death as his father died at the early age. When the family was mourning, Ramana had left. Death gave him questions.

Most important one was Who Am I? One that makes Siddhartha, The Gautama Buddha.

She was on the way to home. Blooming with happiness and excitement. Her mother was to arrive today. They have had arguments, communication gap, and misunderstanding between them for years. She was trying to remember when was the time she spoke her heart out with her mom? She reaches and finds the lady standing at the door, waiting for her with her arms open. She runs and hugs her tight. They go inside, she like the girl in the pink frock, walks tip-toes.

Makes her mother sit on the bed and rests her head on her lap. She kisses her hand and makes her pat her head. She falls asleep.

---

She woke up on the buzz of vibrating phone to find her pillow wet by her tears. She was feeling different, wanted to enjoy the peace that she could feel within her, she completes the call.

Goes back in her dream, finds herself alive after long time. Her heart throbbing with love and compassion. The conscience that tells her that she is a part of existence. The intimate part that has possibility to find the marvellous and significant phenomena within her.

The uncertainty also has something certain in it and today she is aware of that.

It was time to go home and see her mother. Forgive everyone and most importantly, forgive yourself.

The most harm she did to someone in this journey is she herself.

The two tiny drops flowing from her eyes were not actually the pain. It was the remembrance of that unseen she found within. The prayer that probably she never offered, was simply answered.

However, the Khoj will continue forever as it is never ending. The day quest saturates, you are dead. You have lost an opportunity of connecting with the existence. The dialogue, which could have happened with self, will stop.

# FOOT PRINTS

Wherever we go, the Shadow follows

In the shinning sun, we walk together,

In the brighter moon, the shadow merges in us,

We are always guarded, protected by the unknown,

Just this belief that HE there is what you need to live

 Leaving the mark of our presence

Let's carve some foot prints at the ocean shore

Let's celebrate the vulnerability,

Let's assent the power that's hidden in fragility,

Every breath, inhale gratitude and exhale affirmation,

Yet be open to stay curious and alert,

Be open to your Quintessential Quest

The search- Khoj, shall continue.

# GRATITUDE

Once a Sufi Saint was silently passing by a desert with his disciples. It was such a place where this saint was not liked by people. So he and his disciples were captured by the people of the village in that hot desert. Days passed by and the Saint and his disciples were not served with a drop of water or morsel of food.

Disciples started getting angry on their master as they saw him praying and remembering the almighty in that worsened situation as well.

Finally they lost the patience and asked their master, why is he still remembering the lord when he is not there to help him. They may die like this shortly. On the master says, did I question him when we had bowl full of favourite meal?

He is certainly planning for something good.

This story probably is an answer to her and our questions like why me?

# चिट्ठी

इस पिंजर के तहखाने की आखरी सीढ़ी तक, आओगे जब तुम
एक आह मिलेगी और मिलेगा एक सब्र, जिसने बांध के रखे है आस के फेरे,
मूंद के रखा एक कतरा सांस का हथेली में,
ना, रुकना मत, इंतजार है मुझे उस कतरे को लुटा कर,
तुम्हारे साथ चलने का
इस पिंजर से मुक्त, इस तहखाने से उन्मुक्त.

Dear Readers,

This is my first attempt to put forth my perspective of Life, Love, Emotions and Death and most importantly the Questions.

You may find disorientation of thoughts somewhere and repetition of emotions. This book is not planned and written.

As here we are talking of emotions, you may find repetition as ultimately, all emotions come to one and the entire quest leads to one direction.

Would be glad to hear from you. Please feel free to write to a.sristi@gmail.com